BREAD OF LIFE CAFE

By Roger Deloach

Illustrated by Kadin Deloach Kubat

Dedicated to little hungry hearts.

The Bread of Life Café

Published by:
CDM Productions
P.O. Box 161401
Duluth, MN.
(www.cdmproductions.net)

Printed in the United States of America
The Bread of Life Café

First Edition
10 9 8 7 6 5 4 3 2 1

ISBN: 978-0-578-57304-5

The Beginning

Jesus said to them, "I am the bread of life; he who comes to Me shall not hunger, and he who believes in Me shall never thirst."

John 6:35

I sat here this morning

to be fed.

Maybe you put it in the refrigerator by mistake.

Oh, no. I use my Recipe Book much too often to let it sit on the shelf.

Maybe you put it
on the shelf with
the other books.

Oh, no. I don't use pots and pans
for the food in my **Recipe Book.**

Maybe it's under
the pots and pans.

I know many by heart, but there are some I haven't even learned yet. It's also good to read the ones I know over and over again to make sure I don't forget.

It's a big book and has every recipe I need.

I don't know what I would do without it.

Don't be sad, Chef, I'll be glad to help you find it. What does it look like?

Oh, Arffur, I've lost my Recipe Book. How can I serve my customers without my Recipe Book?

What a beautiful morning. I think I
will stop by the Bread of Life Café and
see what my friend, Chef, is doing.

Introduction

It is a blessing to be able to join with Kadin, my
fifteen year old grandson, in his first opportunity to share his
artistic talent in a way that will sow seeds of truth in young im-
pressionable minds.

Kadin and I know that scripture is the ultimate source of
nourishment for every spiritual truth, but at times a warm lap, a
gentle voice, and a willing spirit with a children's book in hand
can provide a wonderful teaching moment that will point the
way to the Bread of Life. It is our hope that this little book will
be a seed planted in a garden that will one day be
harvested in the Kingdom of Heaven.